D1301911

TO:

FROM:

REVOLUTIONIZE
TEAM
WORK

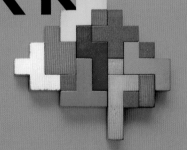

How to Create and Lead Accountable Teams

Eric Coryell

simple **truths**
Small books. BIG IMPACT.

IGNITEREADS
spark impact in just one hour

Published by Simple Truths, an imprint of Sourcebooks, Inc.
P.O. Box 4410, Naperville, Illinois 60567-4410
(630) 961-3900
Fax: (630) 961-2168
sourcebooks.com

Library of Congress Cataloging-in-Publication data is on file with the
publisher.

Printed and bound in China.
OGP 10 9 8 7 6 5 4 3 2 1

This is dedicated to all the people who go to work every day, trying to make their teams and the world a better place. Keep fighting the good fight.

Contents

Introduction

AS AN ORGANIZATIONAL COACH, I am often approached by people seeking advice as to how to get their teams to function better. When I ask them what *function better* means to them, I get a variety of answers, such as "I wish they would think for themselves and not always be looking to me for the answers," or "If they would only stop throwing each other under the bus...," or "I want them to be more accountable," or "I wish they would say what they really feel and not be so afraid of conflict." Concurrently, I am approached by team members looking for advice on what do to when they have *that* boss. The list of issues here is equally diverse. "They are too dictatorial," or "They are too soft and won't hold people accountable," or the opposite, "I wish they would stop micromanaging everything." After having been a part of, led, and worked with countless teams of all sizes in all sorts of industries, I have come to one definitive conclusion: despite the good intent of good people, most teams are dysfunctional.

Everyone wants to be part of a functional team, whether that team is a work team, a sports team, or even a family. Teams have been studied, researched, and written about for decades, but no silver bullet has been discovered. Some books focus on the science of a team, while others focus on the human element. Others have examined a high-performing team in one environment, dissected its key attributes, and then applied those attributes to teams in other environments. These approaches have all served to advance our understanding of teams and how to improve their effectiveness. But despite all that we now know about teams, the nonfunctional teams still far outnumber the functional ones. And as rare as functional teams are, truly accountable teams are rarer still.

This book is written for those people who are struggling to get the team they are leading or the team they are a part of on track. The journey to becoming an accountable team requires taking a road less traveled. Getting there requires thought and behavior that fly in the face of conventional wisdom. In the following chapters, some of what you will read may make you feel a little uncomfortable. You may not agree with some of it. I would like to encourage you, however, to read with an open mind and be willing to challenge some of your current beliefs about teams. Understand that what I am going to talk about is a journey. It takes time. It takes work. And it takes courage. My goal is to share what I have learned that will help you on your own journey. I want to share some of the insight and the tools that I have discovered through the years in the hope that they will make it easier for you to create and lead an accountable team.

1.

Organizational Structure, Teams, and Accountability

PRETEND FOR A MOMENT that you own a company and everybody there reports directly to you. What would you like about that? Almost every answer I hear can be summarized in one word: control. Most people like having and being in control. But there is a downside to control: responsibility. While there are lots of positive emotions around the notion of being in control, the responsibility that comes with it can be exhausting. Imagine now that your company grows, and it becomes increasingly difficult for you to maintain control and shoulder all that responsibility. Departments get added. Layers start to build. Control and responsibility become dispersed throughout the organization. Next thing you know, your organizational chart ends up looking something like what you see in Figure 1.

Figure 1: Business Organizational Chart

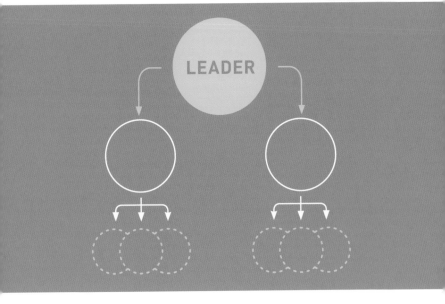

This structure is typical of almost all businesses. Yet it wasn't conceived by a businessperson. It was developed by the Roman military. This model wasn't adopted by businesses until the early 1900s as companies started to grow in size, and it has been the norm ever since.

Figure 2: Military Organizational Chart

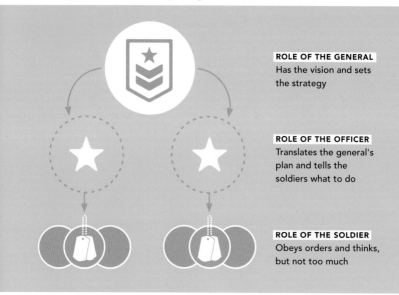

ROLE OF THE GENERAL
Has the vision and sets the strategy

ROLE OF THE OFFICER
Translates the general's plan and tells the soldiers what to do

ROLE OF THE SOLDIER
Obeys orders and thinks, but not too much

From a military perspective, this structure can be broken into four levels. From top to bottom, you have generals, officers, soldiers, and below that, the enemy. The generals' primary role is to do the thinking. They are responsible for creating the vision and the strategy. The officers' primary role is to do the telling. They are responsible for taking the vision and the strategy from the generals, translating it into actionable steps, and then communicating those to the soldiers. But their job does not end there. Once they tell the soldiers what to do, the officers have to verify that the soldiers actually did what they were supposed to. In other words, they have to hold the soldiers accountable. The soldiers' primary purpose is to do what they are told. This structure works because it enables the generals and the officers to ensure that the things they want done get done—and when they don't, they can step in and take control until the desired results are achieved. I call this structure the **Hold Accountable Model**.

THE "HOLD ACCOUNTABLE" MYTH

One of the first things I was told when I became a supervisor was that it was my job to hold my direct reports accountable. It sounded simple enough. And yet it wasn't. I tried many different strategies to get them to do what I thought was necessary, and while some of them seemed to work some of the time, none of them worked all the time. I began to realize it wasn't that simple. I now believe that it isn't even possible.

Let's start with what it means to be accountable. In the simplest terms, accountability is doing what is expected of you or doing what you said you were going to do within a stated time frame. If you meet the expectations set before you, you are being accountable to those expectations.

However, if you fall short of those expectations, you can act in one of two ways: you can act in a way that is unaccountable, or you can act in a way that is accountable.

◆ **Unaccountable behavior:** Make excuses, blame others, deflect, hide, or continue doing the same things over and over, expecting different results.

◆ **Accountable behavior:** Own the fact that you are not meeting expectations and start doing things differently until you meet the desired expectations.

If we can agree that is what accountability looks like, then how does one hold someone accountable? For the leader, the typical process looks something like this:

◆ **Set very clear expectations.**
◆ **Make sure the team member has the skills, tools, and resources necessary to achieve those expectations.**
◆ **Inspire, offer incentives, or set consequences in an effort to motivate the team member.**

◆ **Monitor and measure progress toward meeting those expectations.**

If at this point, the leader discovers that expectations are not being met, he or she can:

◆ **Seek to understand what the problems are.**
◆ **Provide coaching or training.**
◆ **Remove obstacles.**
◆ **Help the team member use problem solving to tackle their difficulties.**
◆ **Find new ways to motivate them.**

If none of these tactics work and an employee continues to fall short of meeting his or her account-abilities, the last remaining option becomes to fire the team member and hire someone new, and the fun starts all over again.

In looking back through all these steps, an interesting question arises: Who was the one being accountable? Who was the one doing something different until the desired results were achieved? **The leader!** The notion of "holding someone accountable" is really a myth. When someone says they are going to "hold someone accountable," what they are really saying is that they are taking the accountability away from that individual and putting it on themselves.

This isn't necessarily a bad thing. The thinking, telling, and doing model has worked to varying degrees throughout history, but the easier and faster transmission of information has changed everything. In today's military landscape, where the enemy has access to more information and can mobilize and redeploy resources quickly, everyone must be able to make faster decisions and respond equally as quickly. There isn't always the time for information to move up the hierarchy to where the decisions are usually made. This has led to the advent of elite military teams such as the U.S. Navy SEALs, who are empowered to make decisions and take on higher levels of

accountability and responsibility closer to where the action is.

The business world has changed too. The speed of business has increased exponentially. I remember when the first company I worked for bought a fax machine. We all stood around it wondering what it was and why anyone would need to transmit information that quickly. That wasn't that long ago. (Okay, so maybe it was.) Today, businesses have extraordinary amounts of information to digest. Customer demand continually changes and evolves. Businesses exist in a constantly shifting competitive landscape in a world where everyone wants everything yesterday. Much as in the military, business leaders are looking to their front-line employees to do more than the doing. They need them to make decisions and take on higher levels of accountability and responsibility while working better with one another to provide a better deliverable more efficiently. An increasing number of business leaders are focusing on employee engagement, the voice of the customer, and the importance of teamwork in their organizations. Despite these efforts, most leaders remain frustrated with the lack of teamwork and agility and the inability to successfully move accountability down into their organizations.

To understand why these efforts struggle to influence the desired changes, you need look no further than the individual employees. One of our core needs as humans is to survive. While meeting the needs of customers and teammates is important, survival at work requires meeting the expectations of the boss. It is the boss who sets the expectations that need to be met, who determines whether an employee keeps his or her job when times are tough, who influences what kind of raise the employee will get when times are good, and ultimately it is the boss who takes the accountability from the employee. As a result, the employee's most important direction to look is up to the leader. This creates a very upward-looking organization, with everyone's backs facing the customer!

So the question now becomes: How? How do you create a more agile, customer-facing organization where employees work together to deliver a better, more efficient outcome for the customer *and* still manage accountability? The answer: create account- able teams. As teams become accountable, they will figure out who their customer is (either internal or external). When things go wrong, they will look to one another and not up to the boss to take care of things. Accountability is no longer always managed by the boss, so the team members stop looking up the organization chart so much.

If only it were that simple. If it were, there would be many more functioning and accountable teams in this world. But they are few and far between. I want to share a road map of what it takes for a team to become accountable and a look at some of the inherent barriers that must be overcome along the way. We are going to start by addressing two of the biggest hurdles on the journey toward team accountability:

1 The leader's unwillingness or inability to let go of the control

2 The team member's unwillingness or inability to take on the accountability

As we already discovered, when an individual fails to be accountable, it is usually the leader who steps in and takes the accountability. On an accountable team, this is done by the team. At first glance, this is a win for the leader, because employees aren't always knocking on the door asking for instructions or permission. The team starts to make more decisions and will begin to focus more on meeting the needs of their customers. This frees the leader up to focus on the bigger picture and longer-term priorities. On the flip side, the leader has to fight the feeling of not being needed or, worst of all, the perception of losing control. For most leaders, the notion of losing control is terrifying.

The good news for the team members is that they

get to be more accountable and responsible. The bad news is…they have to be more accountable and responsible. The typical hierarchical structure creates a lot of parent-child relationships. The boss (parent) will tell the employee what to do. If they do a good job, they get a pat on the back. If they don't do a good job, they get a slap on the hand. And much like at home, if an employee is having problems with one of their teammates (as with a brother or sister), they will often look to the boss (a.k.a. mom or dad) to take care of it. However, as the team becomes accountable, its members have to work out their differences with each other directly. That's called being an **adult**. And quite frankly, it is not always easy being an adult, nor are the accountability and responsibility that come with it.

KEY TAKEAWAYS:

Organizational Structure, Teams, and Accountability

||||||||||||||||||||||||||||||||||||||||||||||||||||||||||||||||||

1. The typical organization hierarchical structure was designed to separate responsibilities and accountabilities into areas of specialization and expertise, which also made it easier for leadership to see where breakdowns were occurring. However, workflow doesn't always move through an organization in the way that structure was designed. Work within most organizations flows sideways across departments rather than top to bottom. Yet accountability tends to be managed in a top-down manner, which often leads to friction and frustration between people in different departments.

2. In the traditional hierarchical structure, leadership assigns different responsibilities to different people and then holds them accountable for meeting those

expectations. What "holding them accountable" really means, however, is that the leader will step in and take the accountability away from the individual or team if they fail to meet expectations. This helps minimize the leader's anxiety, but he or she ends up exhausted from carrying the load. Meanwhile, team members have less anxiety but end up feeling disempowered and disengaged.

3. If the team manages the accountability (i.e. becomes an accountable team), the leader loses some control and the feeling of importance but ends up with more time to focus on long-term work and is no longer the constraint. Meanwhile, the team has the higher levels of anxiety that come with having more accountability and responsibility, but they are empowered and become more engaged.

2.

The Three Types of Teams

IN BUSINESS, WHEN SEVERAL individuals report to the same person, the tendency is to call those individuals a team. Unfortunately, having a group of individuals work for the same person does not ensure they will function as a team. To the contrary, most teams inside organizations are nonfunctional. Good people with good intent, but if you objectively observed their behavior, you would be hard-pressed to describe them as a functioning team. What does a functional team look like? Chances are, you already know. Take a moment and think of the best team you have ever been part of.

It could be your family, a sports team you were on, an organization you volunteered with, or even a team at work. Think about, or better yet, write down what made that team so great. Be specific as you think or write about these things.

I am willing to bet that almost everything you thought of (or wrote down) can be grouped into one of the following seven categories. The first five are required for a team to become functional. The next is what separates accountable from functional teams. Combine all of these, and you will get the ultimate outcome, which is the seventh characteristic.

FUNCTIONAL TEAMS

As you read through each of the following character-istics, think about both your best team and a current team that you are on, and ask yourself if you did (or do) have these:

1   **A clear and commonly accepted purpose.** In order for a team to function well, everyone must have a very clear understanding of exactly what the team is accountable for. Maybe it's to hit a deadline, win the championship, have fun, or achieve a certain measurable goal. Odds are that on your best team, everybody knew exactly what the team's purpose was. Odds are that at least some members of your current team don't. The next time you are together

with your current team, ask each team member to pull out a blank sheet of paper and have them write down what they think the team is accountable for. Very rarely do the answers come close to matching, and if that's the case for your team, you need to take the time to agree on this before you do anything else. You cannot have a functional or accountable team if there is no clear agreement on what the team is accountable for.

2 **A way of determining (measuring) whether or not the team is achieving its purpose.** A team cannot be accountable if its members don't know whether they are successfully achieving their purpose. If they are falling short of expectations, they need to know so they can start doing something differently until the desired results are achieved. Again, go back to your best team. You knew at all points in time if you were on track or not. Now think about your current team and ask yourself, does everyone know?

3 **Competent people.** I have yet to experience a functional team that tolerated incompetence. At the same time, I rarely hear people describe their best teams as having had a bunch of superstars. Instead, they talk about their best team as filled with individuals who were passionate, dedicated, capable, and had a diversity of talent. They knew each other's strengths and weaknesses, and their ability to combine those talents helped them to be great. Is your team made up of competent people working competently together?

4 **Capable processes.** In order for a team to successfully achieve its purpose, its members need good communication, clearly defined roles and responsibilities, good problem-solving processes, and clarity about which decisions they can and cannot make. These are all processes that are vital to a team's ability to function well. Broken or absent processes severely inhibit a team's ability to function. Of all

the characteristics of functional teams, this one seems to get the most time and attention. And it is not even the most important characteristic...

5   **SHARED FATE.** Yes, that is all capitals for a reason. The most important thing a functional team can have is a shared fate. In fact, what makes a team a team is the existence of a real and meaningful shared fate. A shared fate exists when what happens to one happens to all. It means my success (or failure) is tied to your success (or failure). Under pressure, a team without a real or meaningful shared fate will fracture. Team members will worry first about themselves, and the team will break down.

In sports, when someone is late for practice, who runs? Everybody! Shared fate. When the team loses, who loses? Everybody! Shared fate. When a winning basket is made at the buzzer, who celebrates? Everybody! Shared fate.

In the military, high levels of teamwork are

vital for survival, and everyone must go through basic training before they begin. Basic training is designed to teach the soldiers what it means to be a great teammate and how to become one. I once asked a friend who served as a Marine what basic training was like. He told me that while it is different everywhere you go, the objective is always the same: to break you down and connect you with your fellow soldiers. He said he figured this out the second day of boot camp.

"What happened?" I inquired.

"Well, that morning, the sergeant came into the barracks at 0500, woke us all up, and took us down to the beach. There, he advised us that we were all to complete the marked course as fast as we possibly could. It turned out to be a ninety-minute physical gauntlet during which we swam to the point of almost drowning, ran forever, climbed walls, crawled under wire, and then labored around and around an obstacle course in the woods until we finally finished. And you know what? I finished first."

"Wow! That's awesome!" I was impressed.

"No, it wasn't."

"Why not?" I asked, puzzled. After all, he'd done exactly what the sergeant requested— completed the course as fast he could.

"Well, when we were done, they lined us up in the order of our finish. The sergeant got a few inches from my face and proceeded to berate me for about five minutes—although it felt more like half an hour."

"I don't get it."

"Because I passed up all my teammates who were struggling, and I kept going. I figured out in that moment that it didn't really matter when I finished; it only mattered when everyone else finished. That's what they did during basic training. They made your life increasingly miserable until you learned this lesson to your core, and if you didn't, they got you out." Shared fate.

There are all sorts of ways to create shared fate. Making it hard to get on the team creates shared fate. Successfully achieving a goal or a set of metrics as a team creates shared fate. Locating team members' desks close to each other creates shared fate. Pressure situations, difficult conversations, a common enemy, a shared set of values, deadlines, compensation, high stakes, and doing meaningful work are all things that can create a shared fate.

It starts with how the leader views the team. Most leaders think of a team's members as each having separate accountabilities, treat them that way, and then wonder why the group isn't functioning well as a team. To do the things necessary to build a shared fate, the leader must think of the team as a group of individuals who exist to achieve a common account-ability. They will still have separate roles and respon-sibilities, but what really matters is that the team successfully achieves its common purpose.

A shared fate is the engine of every team.

Without it, no team will function under pressure, and its members have little to no chance of ever being an accountable team. Your *best* team had a shared fate. **Does your current team?**

ACCOUNTABLE TEAMS

Just because a team is functional does not mean it will be accountable. A leader can still have all the accountability on a functional team. Surprisingly, in order for a functional team to become accountable, only one thing needs to happen.

6 **Accountable teams deal with their real issues together.** A "real issue" is any issue that affects the team's ability to be successful. If a team is to be accountable (remember our definition of accountability), *the team members* must do something differently until the desired results are achieved. Go back to your best team. When something (or someone) got in the way of you achieving your

goal, did you ignore it? Did you talk behind each other's backs? Did you sit around waiting for the boss, coach, or leader to solve all your problems? I am guessing you didn't. Instead, you talked to one another. You worked through your real issues. Sometimes one-on-one. Sometimes as a group. Sometimes there was even, *gasp*, conflict! Yet most teams don't do this. Most teams work really hard to avoid talking about their real issues. They actually collude not to. Team members talk about the real issues in the bathrooms, bars, or hallways but not when they get together in a meeting. As a result, most people leave a meeting thinking that it was a waste of time. This is in fact often the case. During most meetings, people work hard to not talk about what is real and instead choose to remain silent or focus on other things that are "safer" but not as important to the team's success. Think about your current team and ask yourself how often the team takes on the tough stuff. How often do they enter into real and sometimes difficult discussions? Working through the very issues that feel like they can tear the group apart are the very ones that will bring the group closer together and make it accountable.

The good news is that once team members get good at working through their real issues together, they reap all the benefits. Most notably…

7 **There is an individual commitment to each other's success. The We > I.** When you were on your best team, did you care just as much about your teammates' success as you did your own? I'll bet you did. I will also bet there was a high level of trust among the team members. Team members respected each other, had each other's backs, encouraged each other, and even picked each other up when someone was struggling. Team success became more important than individual success. When a team gets to that point, it becomes its

competition's worst nightmare. Team members develop a swagger. They have an edge. They almost seem to say, "We are going to take over the world." Being on a team like this is an unbelievable experience. Wouldn't it be great if the team you spend most of your time with functioned this way? It can

happen. But it doesn't just happen because someone wishes it would. It happens if you work through the six steps identified above and you engage in the right behaviors. That's what we will examine next.

KEY TAKEAWAYS:

Nonfunctional vs. Functional vs. Accountable Teams

1. Teams can be characterized in one of three ways: nonfunctional, functional, and accountable. Of these three, nonfunctional is by far the most common.

2. You can best tell which category your team falls into by observing it during high-pressure or high-anxiety situations. Nonfunctional teams tend to fracture when its members focus mostly on themselves; some may even throw their teammates under the bus in an effort of self-preservation. Functional teams stick together but will become dependent on their leader to get them through the tough stuff.

---

3. Accountable teams take on the issues that are getting in the way of their success and work through those issues together. Team success far outweighs individual success.

The road to an accountable team requires:

◆ A clear purpose. A team must have a crystal-clear strategy to succeed, and it is ultimately the leader's responsibility to decide what the team is accountable for.

◆ Some way (usually a set of the metrics) that lets team members know they are successfully achieving their accountabilities. They must have a high degree of influence over these metrics, no more than five, and should meet regularly (ideally weekly) to take corrective action when the desired results are not being met.

◆ Competent people.

◆ Capable processes.

◆ A real and meaningful shared fate. A shared fate is created when what happens to one happens to all. High levels of shared fate will keep a team together under pressure.

◆ Ability to work though their real issues together. A real issue is any issue that affects the team's ability to achieve its purpose. Most teams work hard to not talk about these issues. Accountable teams do.

3.

The Behaviors That Matter

SO WHY DO TEAMS tend to avoid dealing with their real issues? The answer is rooted in basic human psychology. One of our strongest biological needs is to be connected to other people. As an infant, this connection is predominantly physical. Babies need to be physically held enough during their early months or they will suffer anaclitic depression, which in some cases can lead to death. As adults, the need for connection is more of an emotional one. Without that connection, people will become depressed and can lose their will to live. As a result, we go to great lengths to avoid separation from people or groups that are important to us.

If you want proof, just go back to high school. How many times did you say something or do something that you didn't really want to say or do, but you did just to stay in good stead with a group that was important to you? If you don't remember, just pay attention to the behavior of some teenagers you know and watch all that they do to stay connected to their groups. We do this as adults as well—we are just a little more sophisticated about it. It explains what happens when the boss walks in the room and suggests a new idea that you don't think is a particularly good one. (Here we go again!) But expressing your concern rarely happens (at least not in the room at the time), and since that disagreement is not expressed, the team agrees to move forward with the idea. Why? Because you (and everyone else) don't want to experience separation. You don't want to be deemed a non–team player, ostracized, devalued, or worse, fired. The risk of any emotional or physical separation is too great, so the real issues are avoided.

This fear of separation leads to a psychological contract that exists on most teams, and it is this contract that keeps real issues from being discussed. The psychological contract that does all the damage goes as follows: *I will not talk about your performance, and you won't talk about mine.* It is an unspoken ("psychological") rule ("contract") that exists on most teams. If someone were to make mention of your nonperformance on a team (they've just broken the contract), you would feel betrayed ("How dare you!"), and you will likely get defensive or counterattack. To prevent this from actually happening to you, you uphold your end of the deal by not talking about them or whatever issue really needs to be talked about. That way, you are safe, since no one can talk about you without breaking the contract.

Let's pretend you have a teammate who is struggling. They are not performing their job well, or they are acting in a way that is detrimental to the team. How do most teams deal with a real issue like this? It is usually a three-step process:

1   **Ignore or avoid the issue.** If someone on the team is struggling to perform, the first tendency is to do nothing. The hope is that the problem will go away or get better on its own. The initial anxiety of addressing the issue is too great. But when things don't get better, the anxiety starts to build, and the next step is to…

2   **Talk behind the person's back.** To minimize their anxiety, team members will turn to other team members and discuss the issue with them. This feels good in the moment! Team members do this to build themselves up or to create a connection with one another, but discussing the issue doesn't solve it. Eventually, the anxiety will start to build again. Next, the team will look for and expect that…

3 **The boss steps up and deals with the issue.** The boss takes the accountability. If the leader effectively deals with the issue, the next time the team has an issue, they will follow the same pattern and become increasingly dependent on the boss. If the boss fails to properly address the issue, the team will start to turn on him or her. Continued failure by the boss will lead to either a mutiny by the team or the team completely shutting down on the boss. Either way, dysfunction sets in!

Tremendous amounts of time, energy, and effort are wasted on these three steps. Worst of all, these three behaviors destroy trust. If I am your teammate, and every time there is a real issue, I just ignore it or turn a blind eye to it, you won't really trust me. If I talk behind your back or even someone else's, you won't trust me. Nor will you trust me if every time a real issue arises, I go running to the boss's office. All three of these behaviors lead to the demise and dysfunction of families, teams, and cultures, because they undermine trust. But there is another option…

1 **The team addresses their real issues together.** This is what functional and accountable teams do. The team members work through their real issues together without engaging in steps one through three above.

Why might it be advantageous for team members to work through their real issues together? Think about your best team again. I will submit that you realized many of the following advantages every time you worked through a real issue together:

◆ **There were more voices on each issue.** There were more data and more perspectives on the table, which helped the team work through the issue.

◆ **There was increased transparency.** Everyone heard the same thing. There was less "he said, she said" on the team.

◆ **It helped validate the issue.** The team was able to determine if the issue was a real one, and it became more difficult for any one member to deflect or deny the issue.

- **It gave everyone on the team a chance to contribute.** This ultimately built a sense of shared fate among the team members.

- **The team became supportive.** It reduced the amount of time spent ignoring and talking about issues behind each other's backs.

- **It helped the team set clear expectations.** Working though real issues made the group norms and boundaries clearer.

- **The team could better address the issue with problem solving.** For starters, the team was able to better identify what the actual issue was. Secondly, the team was able to generate more options for solutions.

- **The team built their problem-solving muscle.** Team members got better and better at working through their own issues. There was increased accountability related to whatever solution the team developed.

◆ **Group learning took place.** Everyone learned from working through the issue together.

◆ **Trust increased, and the team became stronger.** Every time you successfully worked through an issue together, I will bet you found that trust went up and the team became stronger. Not only that, but fear of separation went down! It became safer and safer to be on the team.

If all these advantages come from having the team address their real issues together, why is this approach so rare? Why does the thought of doing this make most people's stomachs turn? It all comes down to the psychological contract and fear of separation. Dealing with real issues together will break the contract, and you may be thinking, "What happens if *I* am the real issue?"

So the question that has plagued me for years is "Why do some teams (like your best team) address their real issues together, while most teams work so hard not to?" What separates the two? What has to exist so that teams will deal with their real issues together and therefore become an accountable team? I think it comes down to two things:

1 A shared fate

2 Meaningful levels of trust

A shared fate is necessary because unless my success or failure is somehow tied to your success or failure, I am not likely to want to break the psychological contract. Instead, I will worry most about myself.

The second thing is trust. If you *really* trusted your teammates and you knew their intention was to help the team succeed or for you to get better or both, would this seem so scary? No. Sure, we all have egos and don't like to be told we're not perfect, but it is pretty easy to get over that when you know that everyone on the team is just trying to help you or the team succeed.

TRUST

We have already talked about shared fate, so let's turn our attention to trust. Trust is the foundation of all teams, and without it, they cannot perform well. I spend a lot of time working with teams where the trust has been severely damaged. What I have discovered is that this breakdown usually occurs when team members interact with one another in destructive ways. There are two behaviors that I am convinced do most of the damage. The first takes place when people talk behind each other's backs before they address a real issue. The second occurs when people don't speak on their own behalf when working through an issue together.

No behavior is more destructive to teams than talking about a real issue without the people affected by that issue involved in its resolution (for example, talking behind each other's backs). If you think about it, talking about an issue without including the member(s) involved doesn't solve the problem. People do it to feel better about themselves, create a connection with the other person, or gather insight or additional data before working though the real issue. At first blush, there are benefits to this behavior, but they all come with significant long-term negative consequences that far outweigh any perceived short-term gain.

In the moment, your anxiety may be reduced when you realize that other people may agree with your perspective, but going home after talking negatively about your teammates does not make you feel inspired or excited about coming to work the next day. One could argue that these conversations can build a connection with the person you are talking to. However, underneath any connection that can be built, trust takes a hit.

In fact, every time you talk negatively about someone behind their back, you become untrustworthy. Deep down, the other person realizes that you would do it to them if the situation warranted that. They will become more guarded around you, and trust will go down.

Another significant consequence of talking about an issue behind someone's back before working it through with the person is that it reduces your ability to effectively work through the issue when it comes time to do so. Most people will justify talking about an issue behind someone's back as a way to gain understanding or additional data before confronting the issue. They want to validate their thoughts before taking the issue on. This really is done because the ego wants to protect itself, to make sure it is right. The problem with having to be "right" before working through the issue is that it means the other person becomes "wrong." Who do you know that likes to be told they are wrong? Nobody. *Every destructive confrontation you have ever been a part of, from an intervention to a feeding frenzy, started with people talking behind each other's backs.*

Teams can work through their real issues together well if everyone comes to the table with their piece of the truth. Then they all must work hard to understand one another's truths to eventually arrive at a shared truth. Discussing the issue in any fashion with a subgroup before working on it as a team totally preempts the team's ability to effectively work through the real issue together in a healthy manner. Doing so also leads to the second destructive behavior that destroys trust: not speaking for yourself.

Trust breaks down on a team when judgment takes place. Most people can handle difficult conversations as long as they know that the other team members have their best interest at heart and aren't thinking less of them as a person when they address an issue.

Most judgment takes place when people don't speak for themselves. Imagine if someone turned to you during a meeting and said, "We have noticed you

haven't been very engaged in the meetings lately. We are wondering if what is being talked about isn't that important to you. When we sense you checking out during the meeting, we have a difficult time maintaining our own levels of concentration and focus." Compare how that feels to someone saying to you, "I have noticed you haven't been very engaged in the meetings lately. I am wondering if what is being talked about isn't that important to you. When I sense you checking out during the meeting, I have a difficult time maintaining my own levels of concentration and focus." Feel the difference? With the first scenario, the person has obviously talked behind your back prior to the meeting, and it is almost impossible not to feel judged and ganged up on. Damage done.

There are two principles that you need to follow and enforce during your meetings to ensure that people are speaking for themselves. The first way people avoid talking for themselves is through the use of group pronouns such as *we, they, our, anybody,* or *everybody.*

In fact, people use group pronouns as a way of not talking about the real issue. Listen for it. You will constantly hear statements like "You know what our problem is? Our problem is that we don't follow a process."

Who is "we"? People wonder: Does that include them? Does that mean *no one* is following the process? If that's the case, they can say, "I am not following the process, and I don't see anyone else on the team following the process either."

You will hear someone say, "Well, it's them!" "Who's 'them'?" you ask. "Well, you know... Management!" "Who is 'management'?" They will use your company name to describe a behavior or an issue that is clearly not a behavior or an issue for everyone in the company.

Your spouse walks into the kitchen and announces, "We need to do dishes." How often does that really mean the two of you? The word *we* is so convoluted in our language. This is yet another example of using a group pronoun to soften a request. It creates confusion

for the other person, as they have to guess what the *we* really means.

It also creates judgment. When you use a form of *we* when talking, I know you have been talking with someone else about the issue before this, and trust starts to break down. So whenever you hear someone use a group pronoun while you are working through an issue, simply ask them to be specific with who they are referring to. If the we statement is being used to avoid speaking only from their own reference point, ask them to just speak for themselves.

The other more subtle way of not speaking for themselves is by asking a question when it is not actually a question. Most questions are really statements in disguise and are posed as questions so that people don't have to speak for themselves. You will hear someone ask a question like "Don't you think it would be a good idea if...?" as opposed to making a statement asserting "I think it would be a good idea if..." Why is there hesitation to make a statement as opposed to asking

a question? Because if someone makes a statement, they own it and can be rejected. Fear of separation. So instead, they ask a question. Asking a question instead of making a statement is really a passive-aggressive way of not speaking for yourself.

The only time a question should be asked is if it is really a question. The way to ensure this is to require that every question be preceded by a statement. The statement should describe the thought that is leading to the need for the question to be answered. Here are two examples:

"I think this is an idea worth considering." (Statement)

"What do you guys think?" (Question)

or

"I am worried about getting to the airport on time." (Statement)

"How long does it take to get to the airport?" (Question)

You will discover that you have people around you who only ask questions and in doing so bring very little value to the table. Teach them to have a voice. When someone asks a question, politely interrupt them and ask them to make a statement first. You will cut your meeting times in half.

KEY TAKEAWAYS:

The Behaviors That Matter Most

1. Our need for connection with other people transcends all other needs, and as a result, fear of separation drives much of human behavior.

2. Fear of separation leads to the creation of an unspoken rule that says, "I won't talk about your performance, and you won't talk about mine." This contract inhibits teams from dealing with their real issues together.

3. Most teams deal with their real issues by ignoring them, talking behind each other's backs, or looking to the leader to take care of the issues. Over the long run, these behaviors actually increase fear of separation and destroy trust on the team.

4. What motivates a team and makes it safe for team members to process their real issues together is a strong sense of shared fate and high levels of trust.

5. Trust is destroyed when we interact with one another in ways that are judgmental or in positions of being "right" or "wrong."

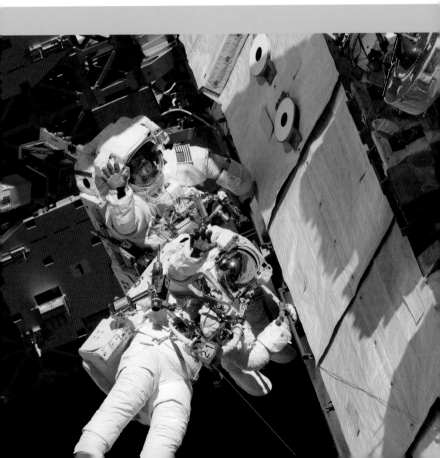

4.

Team Accountability and Decision-Making

WE HAVE TALKED ABOUT how teams typically deal with their issues:

1. Ignore them, avoid them, work around them, or hope they go away.

2. Talk about them behind each other's backs.

3. Look to the leader to solve them (leader has the accountability).

4. Deal with them together as a team (team has the accountability).

You are in the first two phases of dealing with an issue whenever you find yourself dreading going to a meeting, checking out during a meeting, or leaving a meeting feeling as though you just had the life sucked right of you. These are all indicators that the team is working hard to not talk about the real issue(s) at hand and are usually waiting for the leader to step in.

Leaders experience similar feelings during phases one and two. But every leader has only a certain level of anxiety that he or she can tolerate. Once that threshold is reached, they have no choice but to jump in and take control to alleviate their anxiety. At that point, the leader will engage in some fashion and either make the decision or somehow take control of the situation. This pattern can repeat itself for a long time. Eventually, the leader gets frustrated because they feel they are carrying the load, while the group will often feel disempowered and micromanaged.

The irony is that while both sides may complain about it, they both actually love it. The leader has what he or she wants (control), and team members get what they want (to not have to take on the accountability and responsibility). If the team truly wanted accountability and responsibility, team members would leave in search of a leader who would provide that for them. If the leader wanted the team to take on more accountability, they wouldn't tolerate team members not stepping up and taking it. As long as things are working, both sides can comfortably exist with this dynamic.

Problems arise when times get tough. Either the team will turn on the leader, or the leader will turn on the team. If the leader fails to solve all the problems or make the right decisions, the team will get scared and begin to fracture. Team members will blame the leader for their problems and in some cases try to move the leader out. If they are unsuccessful, the team will usually shut down and underperform. If the leader snaps first, he or she will often blame the team for not being accountable and start to engage in efforts to remove the nonperformers. The leader's behavior will become even more dictatorial, and anxiety will rise in the team.

When should the leader take care of the issue, and when should the team? Most sides spend their time and energy pointing at each other. The team watches the leader carefully, and over time, its members start to form opinions about which decisions the leader wants to make and which are theirs. More often than not, they will err on the side of caution and assume the leader wants to do all the decision-making. They will bring the issue to the leader in hopes that he or she will take care of it or provide some level of validation and safety. This is further compounded by the fact that the leader has a hard time not jumping in and taking control to solve the problem because that makes him or her feel better about the job he or she is doing.

One of the most important steps a leader and a team can take is to make very clear which decisions are the team's and which are the leader's. There is a host of processes available to help with this. Two of the more commonly used are RACI and DRIVE. A third is to map out all the decisions that need to be made that affect the team's ability to achieve its purpose and make clear the leader's involvement with each (I call this a decision matrix). For all three, the process is simple. Schedule a three-hour meeting with the team and the leader in a room where you can project what you are typing on the computer to a screen that everyone can see. As a group, build a list of all the significant decisions that have to be made over the course of a year by the leader and the team members who influence the team's ability to achieve its purpose. This is a brainstorming step, so you are going for quantity and not quality, and you will likely generate a list of one to two hundred different decisions.

Once the ideas start to peter out (you will never get a complete list), stop the discussion and codify the list according to what model you choose to use. If you use the RACI model, for each decision, you need to identify who is:

Responsible. **Who owns the decision or problem.**

Accountable. **Who the person or team responsible for making the decision is accountable to when making the decision or solving the problem.**

Consulted. **Who should be consulted in addressing the problem or making the decision.**

Informed. **Who should be informed about the decision or problem resolution.**

The DRIVE model is similar:

Decide. **Who makes the decision.**

Recommend. **Who can recommend options for a decision.**

Input. **Whose input should be consulted for the decision.**

Veto. **Who can challenge or obstruct the decision.**

Execute. **Who will ultimately be acting on or implementing the decision.**

For both of these models, the leader gets the final say, but there is active discussion and input from the team members on their thoughts and needs as well.

The third option is to have the leader codify each of these decisions into one of four categories. Level one decisions are the leader's decisions. So if the decision is to terminate an employee, the leader may decide that that decision is significant enough where they get the final say. Or the leader may determine it to be a level two decision, which means it is the team's or individual team member's decision, but before they make the final decision and act on it, the leader wants to know ahead of time. This gives the leader the opportunity to weigh in or share some perspective before the decision is made, but at the end of the day, it is not the leader's final decision. Or the leader could also assign it to someone else to weigh in on, such as someone in Human Resources. This would imply that, while it is not the final decision of Human Resources, the decision must be run past them to make sure that everything is in line before the decision is acted on.

The leader could classify the decision as a level three decision, which means it is the team's or a team

member's decision, but the leader wants to be made aware of it at some point shortly afterward. Level four decisions are simple: your call and I don't even want to know about it. Once all the decisions are coded, you can sort them by decision level and make sure that what the leader has decided on is in line with what the leader wants the team to be accountable for. If the leader wants the team to be highly accountable yet every decision is a level one decision, the team will have no chance of being successful. The decision level authority given must be congruent with what the team is being asked to be accountable for. See Figure 3 on page 74 for an example of how to organize your level classification chart.

Figure 3: Sample Decision Matrix

John is the leader in this example and is also considered part of the Executive Leadership Team (ELT). Jerry, Jenny, Dan, Bill, and Marry are all part of John's leadership team.

LEVEL ❶ DECISION	Leader's decision
LEVEL ❷ DECISION	Owner's/team member's decision, discuss with leader first but ultimately is the owner's final decision
LEVEL ❸ DECISION	Owner's/team member's decision, but keep leader/accountable entity in the loop at some point
LEVEL ❹ DECISION	Owner's/team member's decision, leader/accountable entity doesn't need to know anything about it

ACCOUNTABLE ENTITY (Level)	DECISION OWNER	DECISION DESCRIPTION
①John ②Jerry	Dan	Change in coverage hours
④John	Jenny	Inventory purchases </= $100,000
②Jerry ④John	Jenny	Inventory purchases > $100,000
②Jerry ④John	Anyone on ELT	Other contracts/purchases > $100,000
①Mary ②Bill ④John	Anyone on ELT	Software purchases/incorporation/non-core software change
①Mary ②Bill ③John	Anyone on ELT	Any major IT infrastructure change
①John ②ELT	Anyone on ELT	Any major HR policy change
②HR ③ELT	Anyone on ELT	Non-ELT firing decision
②ELT	Jerry	Changes to employee benefit offerings
①John ②ELT	Jerry	Office space/new building
②ELT	John	Core system software change

This exercise can also help the leader avoid being perceived as a micromanager or a control freak. When a team member approaches the leader with a decision or a request for input on a decision, the key for the leader is to develop the discipline to ask themselves what level decision it is. If it is a level three or four decision, the leader has to resist the temptation to take it or influence it and instead remind the individual of its agreed upon level. If it is a one or two, the leader can act accordingly and involve themselves in the decision. This decreases the team's dependence on the leader and creates clarity for the team. And clarity creates freedom and empowers the team. If you go back to your best team, I will venture to guess that everyone had a pretty clear idea of what decisions they could and could not make.

This tool will help you at every level of business. You can do this upward with your boss or a board of directors. You can also cascade down through all levels of the organization. The levels may change. As a team demonstrates high levels of accountability, the leader may choose to give them more autonomy and accountability around decisions. If the team struggles with taking accountability, if new, less experienced members join the team, or if times get tough, the leader may decide to draw the reins in a little bit. There is no right or wrong; you are just trying to define reality as it stands and make it clear for everyone. Will you get every decision coded? Unlikely, but if you can get the majority of the major decisions defined and coded, it will create enough context for the team to pick up the rest. Right now, they are spending a lot of time trying to figure it out by watching the leader's every move and reaction and then guessing.

BREAKING THE CONTRACT

Achieving clarity about which issues are the team's and which are the leader's does not guarantee that the team will start having healthy, real-issue discussions. The psychological contract must be broken, or the team's members will struggle to deal with their real issues. Before a team can do this, the habit of talking behind each other's backs must be stopped, and above all, the team must develop the habit of everyone speaking for themselves. In order to do this constructively, a deeper understanding of how to construct a real-issue conversation is necessary.

I started to understand this long ago when a team I was on had a real-issue conversation with one of the team members. But before I get into that story, I have a question I want you to answer. Do you have any performance issues anywhere in the organization that you work in or belong to? I know that is probably something of a rhetorical question, but here is my next question: How

many people do you know who think that they person-
ally have a performance issue? How many people ever
step up and say, "Oh, performance issue? That's me!
Hey, everybody, I am over here! I am the performance
issue." I am guessing the answer to that is close to zero.
Yet that wasn't your answer to how many performance
issues you have at work. Crazy, isn't it?

Well, I had concerns about the performance of a
teammate of mine, "George," who happened to head
the HR department. This particular team was very
functional, and we were in the process of becoming
more accountable. I also felt there was a decent level
of trust, so I shared my concerns during a meeting
that what HR was focusing on wasn't what I thought
they should be. Fortunately, George didn't get too
defensive, and it led to a conversation where we as a
management team agreed on a list of what we thought
the priorities and expectations should be of the HR
department. I have forgotten exactly what was on the
list, but there were things like "There needs to be a

waiting list of people who want to come work here," "All of our employees should have a self-development plan," and so on. What I will never forget was the look on George's face when we were done making the list.

"What?" he uttered in confusion. "I was hired because we were in violation of two state laws, we had no employee handbook, no job descriptions…" Guess what George got done during his first few years on the job? All those things. He was walking around thinking he was a rock star. What had happened to expectations of him? They were so clear when he first started his job, but over time, not only did his boss start having different thoughts, but so did all his peers. These were never really agreed upon or discussed. And then it hit me. What occurred to me in that moment was that the performance conversation (or any real-issue conversation, for that matter) is always a conversation about the gap that exists between expectations and reality.

Figure 4: Performance Conversation Gap

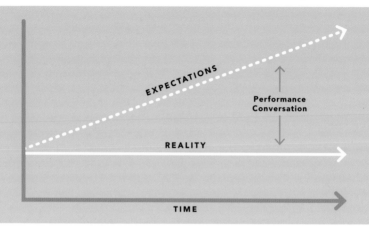

Whenever you have a performance (or real-issue) conversation with someone, you are talking about the gap that exists between your expectations and the reality you are experiencing. "I expect this behavior, and instead, I am seeing that behavior." "I expect these results, and instead, I am seeing those results." The problem is the tendency to put off having the conversation until there is so much frustration over unmet expectations that the discussion tends to go poorly and there are very few options remaining.

This really hit home for me a few weeks later when someone on our team expressed their concern that I wasn't bringing in enough new business in my role in new business development. I must admit I got a little defensive at first, but we ended up having a good conversation about expectations and how those compared to the current reality. We eventually agreed on the expectations going forward and generated some ideas on what needed to be done differently. The real power of this experience, however, occurred to me well after the meeting.

As uncomfortable as the conversation was at the time, I realized that I was on a team that cared enough about me to have the conversation as soon as expectations and reality started to significantly deviate. More importantly, they didn't do what most would have done. Most teams would have ignored the problem. Then when they realized that things weren't getting any better, they would have talked behind my back. Eventually, they would have looked to the boss to take on the issue, and by that time, it's usually a termination discussion. I

started to realize my team really cared about my success and our team's success because they chose to have the conversation with me. And this understanding increased with every subsequent real-issue conversation we had as a team. With each conversation, my level of trust went up, my fear of separation went down, and I was more motivated than ever to do a good job for the team.

Which team would you rather be on? One that works through issues together, or one that ignores them, talks behind each other's backs, and waits for the leader to take care of everything? If you are like most people, you will choose the former. Yet most teams do the latter. It's a paradox made possible by the psychological contract, which is driven by our fear of separation.

As trust begins to build, you can break the psychological contract with the team. The process always starts by agreeing on expectations as a team. On most teams where the leader holds accountability, the only expectations that need to be understood and met by team members are the expectations of the leader. Looking good to the boss is all that matters. In the accountable team model, however, the expectations need to be set by the team, which includes the leader. Here is one of my preferred processes that you can use to break the psychological contract. Follow these steps and reference Figure 5 on pages 86–87 as an example:

1   Start by having everyone individually identify their performance expectations for all members on the team. People will often write down things like: "Be

accountable," "Be competent at your job," "Have a positive attitude," "Share your knowledge," "Have one another's back," etc.

2 Consolidate those expectations on the board or screen, and make sure everyone fully understands the meaning of each one and commits to it being necessary to the team's success. For example, someone could take exception to having a positive attitude. Discuss it until you can settle on something the team can all agree to, like "Have a productive attitude," and define what that means.

3 Once the expectations are agreed upon, start talking about any gaps that exist between those expectations and perceived reality. To begin this step, have someone on the team volunteer to go first. Next, have all the team members (including the volunteer) write down three expectations that they think the volunteer can improve on the most.

4   Tally the results, and have the volunteer pick one item (usually one that garners a lot of the votes) to work on first.

5   The team members need to clearly state their expectations about that item and then describe the reality as they see it. This will help make the gaps between the two very clear.

6   Now it becomes the volunteer's time to participate. He or she starts by asking clarifying questions about the input received. Once that is done, the volunteer completes each of the boxes in Figure 5 with the group's help. This is their commitment to what they are going to do to resolve the gap.

7   Repeat the process starting at step 3 for each member in the group.

Figure 5: Improvement Plans for ABC Company

	WHAT?	REALIZATION	HOW?
	What is the outcome I would like to have?	What has gotten in the way of me not doing this in the past?	What am I going to do differently to make this a reality?
MARY	I want anyone to be able to walk up to me and be able to have a comfortable and normal conversation, even if they are challenging me or I disagree with what they are saying.	My impatience, stubbornness, and my need to be right.	I am going to focus on all these interactions/increase my awareness of my response and change it until it becomes a habit.
BETH			
JOHN			
BILL			
TIM			
ELISE			

BENEFITS	VERIFICATION	RE-EVALUATION
What are the benefits to me/ others of making this change?	**How am I going to know whether the desired improvement/change has been made?**	**When will we check on progress?**
People will feel more listened to and valued, will more freely offer their opinions, and I will learn more and in turn be a more effective leader.	Feedback from all my direct reports. I am going to let them know I am working on this and will solicit their opinion on my progress in two months.	3/12

When you have completed this for each team member, the psychological contract will be broken because everyone will have talked about everybody else's performance within the team. Once the team starts using the process, giving feedback to one another will become easier and easier, until eventually the team won't need a structured process to take members through the conversations.

KEY TAKEAWAYS:

Team Accountability

1. When you find yourself dreading going to team meetings, checking out a lot during those meetings, or leaving them feeling exceptionally drained, that's a pretty good sign that you and the team are avoiding dealing with the real issues.

    On most teams, the real issues will go unaddressed until the group either draws the leader in or the leader steps in and takes the accountability. If the leader does a good job at this, the group increases its dependence on the leader. If the leader fails, the group will eventually turn on him or her.

2. A foundational step on the road toward team accountability is to clearly define the team's levels of authority around making decisions, then determine who is going to be involved in the process and in what capacity. By having these conversations, the leader

can better manage the transition of accountability to the team.

3. In order to get a team to start addressing real issues together, the psychological contract must be broken. But before a group can break that contract, there must be clear performance expectations. Clear expectations are the baseline against which reality is measured to determine if there is a performance gap. Once the gap is identified, it is easier to break the contract and address the real issues.

4. All real-issue conversations are really conversations about the gap between what is expected and what is experienced.

5.

Putting It All Together

IT IS OFTEN A challenge to take a concept on paper and put it into action. Every situation is unique. Stakes are high. The future is fraught with uncertainty. Doing this takes a lot of courage. Staying the course with all its downsides may seem like a safer option than something that sounds good on paper but comes with no guarantees. But to expect things to be different without making changes is an exercise in futility. There are no guarantees that the leader will let go of control. There are no guarantees that the team will step up and be accountable. There are no guarantees that the team will deliver extraordinary results. I am convinced, however, that there are steps you need to take to get there, and successful completion of those steps will greatly increase the chance of success.

All change starts with you. My dad used to say, "You get what you tolerate." For the longest time, I had absolutely no clue what he meant by that. With time, however, I finally understood it. Who you are as a parent, who you are as a leader, who you are as a person is defined greatly by what you do and do not tolerate. Your family, your team, is functioning exactly the way it is based entirely on what you do and do not tolerate. If you want the team you are on or the team you are leading to change, you must change what you tolerate. If you want to start building the necessary levels of trust on your team, you have to stop tolerating the behaviors that destroy trust. No more talking about an issue behind someone's back before bringing it to them. No more speaking on behalf of others when working through an issue. No more asking questions without a statement. You must stop tolerating these behaviors in others and in yourself. Nothing will change until you do.

So what do you want to change? Do you want the team to take on higher levels of accountability and responsibility? Do you want people to start saying what they really feel in meetings? Do you want to build the level of trust on your team? Do you want there to be real dialogue, cross talk, and even conflict on your team? If so, let's take a look at all that we have covered and put it into action. It starts with assessing your own and your team's readiness to be accountable.

Questions I would encourage the leader to answer before starting:

1 **What frightens you most about giving up some control to the team? What is the worst-case scenario for you?** If the team is going to become more accountable, the leader has to give up some

control. I spent years wanting my team to be accountable and at the same time wanting all the control. This doesn't work. Learning to lead in an accountable team environment can be likened to being a coach or a parent. You get to set the deal and decide who gets to decide what, but you can't overstep those bounds. You don't get to be on the field during every play, and you can't sit in the back seat on the way to prom. That's not so easy when you think your job is on the line.

2 **Is there at least one person on the team who you feel is truly accountable and capable of putting the team's purpose ahead of their own?** As discussed in chapter 1 and throughout this book, if a leader is going to let go of some of the accountability, the team has to step up and take it. If there aren't people on the team who are fundamentally accountable in most of their own behavior and able to put the team on at least equal ground with their

own accountability, I might suggest holding off until you can get some people who fill this bill.

3 **How ready do you think your team is to take on higher levels of accountability and responsibility?** Are they asking for it, or will you be pushing it? How dependent are they on the leader now? It is not an easy switch to go from being told what to do to being responsible for your own accountability. The more a team is used to being told what to do and the more the accountability has been taken by the leader, the more difficult this transition will be. It does not make it impossible; it just requires the leader to work really hard to clarify new expectations and make it safe for the team to fail and try again.

4 **What is the level of trust on the team? Are there any relationships that are damaged beyond repair?** Step back and assess the general level of trust on the team. Things to watch for are:

a. **Entrenched Pairs:** *Two or more people who are so close that you know if you speak to one, the other will hear about it. This team within a team can be very damaging to trust and needs to be addressed.*

b. **Orphans:** *One or more individuals who seem to be ostracized by the rest of the team. There is actually a shared fate by distancing themselves from the orphan(s). This leaves you with multiple teams with multiple shared fates that will inhibit the team's ability to function.*

c. **Open Dialogue:** *How often people talk about anything tough in the group setting. If all your meetings are pretty safe and people don't often speak up, that's a good sign that it is not safe on the team and there potentially are some fairly significant trust issues.*

Next, you have to assess if there is a basis for the team to function like an accountable team:

1. **What would you like the team to be accountable for?** This is the team's purpose. I believe what the team should be accountable for is ultimately the leader's decision. What the team is accountable for is different from the company's purpose. It should be easily articulated and describe the *what*, not the *how*. The *how* is a behavior or a process. The *what* is an outcome. If you cannot clearly identify this, then do not proceed until you can.

2. **What are the sources of shared fate for the individuals on this team? In what ways is each team member's success tied to the others' success, and why should they really care?** This is the engine that makes a team function. If you can't identify or create meaningful levels of shared

fate for the team, it will fall apart under duress. As a leader, you will start to build the shared fate when you start treating the group as a team that is accountable for achieving a specific outcome (e.g. the team's purpose) and not as a group of individuals with different accountabilities. If you struggle to identify or envision a meaningful shared fate for the team, I would challenge the assumption that making them an accountable team is the right thing to do.

At this point, metrics need to be developed that tell the team whether it is achieving its purpose/accountabilities. I usually suggest that this be done with the team's help, but it certainly can be done by the leader alone before introducing the metrics to the team.

If metrics are developed with the team, here is the process I would suggest:

1   Articulate what you want the team to be account-
    able for.

2   Engage in conversation with the team around that
    purpose. Ask people what certain parts of the
    purpose mean to them. The goal is to allow every-
    one to take in and digest the purpose and make
    sure there is a common understanding of it, what it
    means and doesn't mean, what the impact is, and
    so on.

3   Agree to a set of criteria for good metrics. Typically:
    a.   *Each metric must be something the team has a high
         degree of influence over.*
    b.   *Each metric must be measurable and updated on a
         timely basis (weekly, or worst case, monthly).*
    c.   *Each metric should be charted on a rolling average*

basis so the group doesn't overreact to one bad data point.

d. Each metric must connect directly to the team's purpose. No sub-metrics.

e. Each metric should have clear criteria for success. Usually, it's good to use the SMART criteria (specific, measurable, achievable, relevant, and time-bound) for the goals that are set.

f. No more than five metrics. Three to four are ideal.

g. When done creating a set of metrics, the team should be able to answer the question, "If we are hitting on all these metrics, is the team achieving its accountability?" There should be a resounding "Yes!"

4   Once the criteria are established, have each team member write down all the possible metrics that they can think of that could in some way measure what the purpose is defined to be. Get these on the board. As a group, whittle them down to five or

fewer, and make sure they each meet your criteria for a good metric.

5   Create an accountability board. Going back to our definition of accountability, if the desired expectations are not being met, the team must take different actions until the expectations are met. The accountability board is designed to be a working board that the team uses to figure out what actions they should take and then measure whether those actions are being achieved.

The team is now taking accountability for their results by identifying and executing on ideas they can do differently to achieve the desired results they are not achieving. The leader can set boundaries around time frames to fix unacceptable results, and they don't have to accept bad answers, but they are no longer taking accountability for the results. If the team continues to fail to deliver on the results, the

leader, of course, will have to step back in and take the accountability.

Many of the real issues the team needs to address will surface as they work the metric board. By definition, a "real issue" is any issue that is affecting the team's ability to be successful, and those issues will more often than not surface during this process. The team can choose not to address them, and that is why it is so important to do this in conjunction with the work identified in chapters 3 and 4, which helps the team build the necessary levels of trust, creates a shared fate, and allows the team to successfully break the psychological contract.

Conclusion

GETTING A TEAM TO operate as an accountable team is a journey. It doesn't happen overnight. Depending on where your team is on its journey, application of some of the tools in this book may seem difficult or overwhelming. As the team makes progress through the initial steps, however, it will become easier for them to tackle some of the more difficult challenges that lie ahead. The good news is that these steps of defining a purpose, devising metrics, and creating a shared fate aren't that difficult; they just take time and attention. The tips in this book about defining a purpose, developing an accountability board, completing a decision matrix, and building a shared fate will help you work through this part of the process.

The more challenging aspects of getting the team to become accountable rest with how team members behave and function together. The need for safety and connection often leads team members to behave in ways that they think *will* best keep them connected to the team. To most people, this means it is best to not rock the boat, challenge authority, or disagree with the general group consensus. Instead, they will express their true feelings with individuals who they deem to be safe and look to the leader to make everything okay. But this behavior undermines trust and the success of the team and actually creates the separation from the team they fear most.

What makes a team accountable is that they choose to work together on the issues that are getting in the way of them delivering on the desired results. Doing this requires real conviction, courage, and trust. The conviction comes from a clear and meaningful purpose and a shared fate among the team members that connects their individual success or failure to those of their teammates and the team. The courage comes from overcoming our inherent fear of separation, which comes from a feeling of connection with a team whose purpose is meaningful to them.

Trust is earned. Trust comes from doing real work together. Trust is built when people speak only for themselves in doing this work. Trust is built when people choose to say what they really feel to their team and not in subgroups or outside the team. As uncomfortable or unconventional as these concepts may seem, they are your secret weapons in building an accountable team.

Acknowledgments

THIS BOOK WOULDN'T HAVE been written without Pat Murray. I first was exposed to Pat and his work early in my first job out of college. In a world inundated with so much information that is often regurgitated or repackaged, Pat is one of the few original thinkers still out there. He ignited my passion for teams, and his teachings have guided me every day since. Through the years, I have incorporated my own lessons and models based on all the failures and triumphs I experienced with teams, but when I was asked to whittle everything down to the few simple truths to write this book, I was struck by how much of what remained I learned from Pat. There are no words that could ever fully express my gratitude for the work he has done and the guidance he has provided me.

Almost every author acknowledgment starts with the statement of "There are too many people to thank and name!" I now fully understand that sentiment. There are so many people who I have learned from through the years that it is impossible to name them all and articulate all that I am grateful for. Thank you to all the people who coached and challenged me in the "early years": George Fox, Bob Winter, Scott Grinna, Scott Wiedenhoeft, and Dennis Gilkey. My greatest team and leadership lessons came from Kurt Bell and the many people I worked with at HUI. Kurt had the courage to try (and to fail!) and try again until it all started to come together. He taught me what it meant to be a leader, a coach, and a friend. I am also most grateful to Dan Ruedinger, Judy Guten, and Dawn Coryell for pushing me out of my comfort zone and encouraging me to go do what I really love even though my ego resisted at every turn. I get to do what I love every day because of you.

There are also so many amazing thought leaders that have influenced me in so many ways. In addition to Pat Murray, Jerry Harvey, Simon Sinek, Mark Manson, Lee Thayer, Len Leritz, and Brené Brown are stalwarts in their ability to see truth and share those truths in ways that are so meaningful. I also want to thank those who worked with me on this book, from encouraging me to write it to reviewing and critiquing the drafts, including Valarie Bartalme, Laura Klocke, Jen Peterson, and my very patient editor, Meg Gibbons.

Finally, to my two greatest teachers: my daughter, Shannon, and wife, Marikris. I am so very proud to be your dad and husband. Thank you for all the gifts and joy you bring me every day.

About the Author

Eric dedicates his working life to helping other leaders engage their employees through the creation of functional and accountable teams. He learned the importance and impact of achieving meaningful levels of trust and accountability in organizations during his "working career," which spanned twenty years across three different manufacturing organizations in Wisconsin. Through the course of these years, Eric held a variety of positions, including two stints as company president, during which he learned a lot about the promises and pitfalls of leadership and leading teams. When not enjoying time with his wife and daughter, Eric is in relentless pursuit of his first hole in one, and he enjoys cycling, the outdoors, hiking, kayaking, and sailing.

NEW! Only from Simple Truths®

IGNITE READS
spark impact in just one hour

IGNITE READS IS A NEW SERIES OF 1-HOUR READS WRITTEN BY WORLD-RENOWNED EXPERTS!

These captivating books will help you become the best version of yourself, allowing for new opportunities in your personal and professional life. Accelerate your career and expand your knowledge with these powerful books written on today's hottest ideas.

TRENDING BUSINESS AND PERSONAL GROWTH TOPICS

Read in an hour or less

Leading experts and authors

Bold design and captivating content